BASKETBALL JOKES

Why did the basketball player have alphabet soup for lunch every day?

So he could eat and practice reading at the same time. ⇨

Coach: *What are you going to be when you grow up?*
Player: *An old man.*

Knock-knock.
Who's there?
Donna.
Donna who?
Donna take all the shots.

New Coach: *Are you chewing gum?*
Player: *No sir, I'm Robert Smith.*

Knock-knock.
Who's there?
Phyllis.
Phyllis who?
Phillis in on what you did all summer.

Coach: *How did you find school today?*
Player: *I just got off the bus, and there it was.*

Did you hear about the player who was so short he had to wear socks to keep his neck warm. ⇦

Sign in coach's office: *If you won't have your hair cut, at least change the oil.*

Knock-knock.
Who's there?
Dozen.
Dozen who?
Dozen anyone know what the score is?

Heard in the locker room: *The only thing he took up in school was space.*

Knock-knock.
Who's there?
Kent.
Kent who?
Kent you let us in on the play?

Just because you dribble all over yourself doesn't make you a basketball player.

What do you call a hot dog that never loses?

A wiener. ⇨

There's a basketball player named
Jordan,
Who has far more moves than Flash
Gordon.
He goes over and around you,
And on defense he'll astound you.
This NBA star, Michael Jordan.

Knock-knock.
Who's there?
Esau.
Esau who?
Esau me miss that free throw.

Teacher: *George, can you name the four
seasons of the year?*
George: *Football, basketball, baseball and
soccer.*

Knock-knock.
Who's there?
Annie.
Annie who?
Annie body need help on defense?

What is a Hawaiian basketball player's favorite shot?

A lei up. ⇦

What did the elementary student put down when asked to list his three favorite sports?
NBA basketball, college basketball and high school basketball.

Knock-knock.
Who's there?
Frank Lee.
Frank Lee who?
Frank Lee I don't know how he missed that shot.

Make like a basketball and bounce out of here.

Knock-knock.
Who's there?
Andy.
Andy who?
Andy fouls on almost every play.

Coach: *Let me give you a piece of my mind.*
Player: *I hope you can spare it.*

Why do basketball players always put their right shoe on first?

Because they don't want to put the wrong shoe on first. ⇨

In a library, where would you find basketball players' autobiographies?
Under tall tales.

Knock-knock.
Who's there?
Auto.
Auto who?
Auto be able to shoot foul shots.

There's a player for Orlando named O'Neal,
Who was given the first name of Shaquille.
But he's better known as Shaq,
And wears thirty-two on his back.
This outstanding star who has such great appeal.

Knock-knock.
Who's there?
Betty.
Betty who?
Betty misses the next shot.

How do the players keep cool at a basketball game?

There are a lot of fans there. ⇦

George: *Will you come to the gym with me?*
Jim: *Why?*
George: *My trainer told me to work out with a dumbbell.*

Knock-knock.
Who's there?
Olive.
Olive who?
Olive right next door to the gym.

Coach: *Son, you've got to stop eating junk food.*
Player: *Do you know where I can find some organic twinkies?*

Knock-knock.
Who's there?
Phil.
Phil who?
Phil up the ball, it needs air.

What was Earl The Pearl's middlename?
The.

What kind of coach has no wheels?
A basketball coach. ⇨

Why won't some basketball players get on the bus?
They don't want to be called for traveling.

Knock-knock.
Who's there?
Imen.
Imen who?
Imen hot water with the coach.

Of all the sports, basketball attracts the highest caliber of kids.

Knock-knock.
Who's there?
Juneau.
Juneau who?
Juneau how much time is left on the clock?

Player: *My wife is one of twins.*
Coach: *How do you tell them apart?*
Player: *Her brother has a beard.*

When is a referee like a bird of prey ?

When he watches you like a hawk. ⇦

What makes the floors of a basketball court wet?
The players . . . they dribble.

What makes the floors even wetter?
The players . . . they double dribble.

Knock-knock.
Who's there?
Yule.
Yule who?
Yule never guess the defense they're playing.

Coach: *Smith, I understand you missed practice yesterday.*
Smith: *No coach, I didn't miss it at all.*

Knock-knock.
Who's there?
Arthur.
Arthur who?
Arthur any plays that will work?

Waiter: *All the food we serve is ala carte.*
Basketball Player: *Then just wheel it on in.* ⇨

Coach: *Can you keep a secret?*
Center: *Yes, but the guys I tell it to can't.*

Knock-knock.
Who's there?
Lettuce.
Lettuce who?
Lettuce score on this play.

New Player: *I'm a little stiff from running.*
Coach: *I don't care if you're from Boston, get out there and loosen up.*

Knock-knock.
Who's there?
Hewlett.
Hewlett who?
Hewlett you on the court?

Coach: *Smith, how do you spell Mississippi?*
Smith: *The river or the state?*

What is a cheerleader's favorite drink?

Root beer. ⟵⟶

Coach: *Smith, do you find you have trouble making decisions?*
Smith: *Well, yes and no.*

Knock-knock.
Who's there?
Hedda.
Hedda who?
Hedda feeling he would score on that drive.

What's the difference between a teacher/coach and a railroad conductor?
One trains the mind and the other minds the train.

Coach: *If can't is short for cannot, what is don't short for?*
Player: *Doughnut.*

Basketball Player: *Dad, when I graduate, what do you suggest I read?*
Dad: *The want ads.*